Christmas Foods

Jenny Vaughan and
Penny Beauchamp

Heinemann Library
Chicago, Illinois

© 2004 Heinemann Library
a division of Reed Elsevier Inc.
Chicago, Illinois

Customer Service 888-454-2279

Visit our website at
www.heinemannlibrary.com

Produced for Heinemann Library by
Discovery Books Ltd.
Designed by Jo Hinton-Malivoire
and Rob Norridge
Illustrations by Nicholas Beresford-Davies
Picture Research by Laura Durman
Originated by Dot Gradations Ltd.
Printed in China by WKT Company Limited

08 07 06 05 04
10 9 8 7 6 5 4 3 2 1

**Library of Congress Cataloging-in-
Publication Data**
Vaughan, Jenny.
  Christmas foods / Jenny Vaughan and
Penny Beauchamp.
      p. cm. -- (A World of recipes)
Summary: Includes easy-to-prepare Christmas
recipes from different cultures around the
world.
  ISBN 1-4034-4697-0 (HC) -- ISBN 1-4034-
6011-6 (pbk.) 1. Christmas cookery--Juvenile
literature. 2. Cookery, International--Juvenile
literature. [1. Christmas cookery. 2. Cookery,
International.] I. Beauchamp, Penny. II. Title.
  TX739.2.C45V38 2004
  641.5'686--dc22

2003018012

Acknowledgments
The author and publishers are grateful to
the following for permission to reproduce
copyright material: p. 5 Regis Bossu/Corbis; p.
6, 24, 25, 30, 31, 32, 33, 34, 35, 36, 37, 38,
39, 40, 41, 42, 43 Steve Lee; p. 10, 11, 12, 13,
14, 15, 16, 17, 18, 19, 20, 21, 22, 23, 26, 27,
28, 29 Terry Benson.

Cover photographs reproduced with
permission of Terry Benson and Steve Lee.

Contents

The History of Christmas 4

Ingredients 6

Before You Start 8

Shrimp Snacks (Philippines) . . . . .10 **

Festive Mushroom Soup (Poland) . . . . .12 **

Chicken and Meatball Soup
   (Palestine) . . . . .14 **

Niños Envueltos (Argentina) . . . . .16 ***

Savory Rice (Brazil) . . . . .18 **

Jansson's Temptation (Sweden) . . . . . .20 **

Mince Pies (England) . . . . .22 *

Ghryba Shortbread (Egypt) . . . . .24 **

Melomakarona (Greece) . . . . .26 **

Stollen (Austria) . . . . .28 ***

Amaretti (Italy) . . . . .30 *

Christmas Cookies (Canada) . . . . .32 *

Christmas Bread (Chile) . . . . .34 **

Turrón (Spain) . . . . .36 **

Candied Sweet Potatoes
   (United States) . . . . .38 **

Christmas Pudding Ice Cream
   (Australia) . . . . .40 *

Spiced Grape Juice (Germany) . . . . . . .42 *

Further Information 44

Healthy Eating 45

Glossary 46

Index .48

Key

* easy

** medium

*** difficult

Some words are shown in bold, **like this.** You can find out what they mean by looking in the glossary.

The History of Christmas

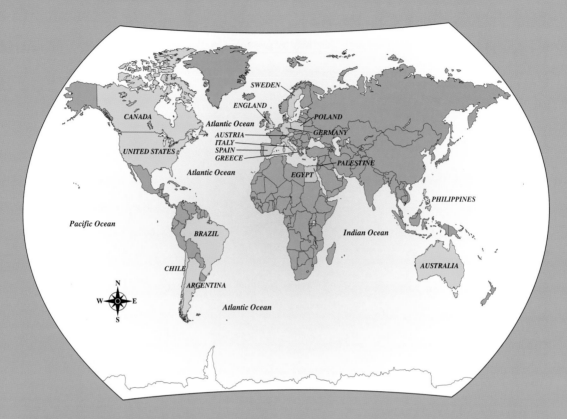

Christmas Day

On Christmas Day Christians celebrate the birth of Jesus Christ, the founder of Christianity. For most Christians, Christmas falls on December 25, but in some places, such as Armenia, it is celebrated on January 6. Christmas is one of the most important Christian festivals of the year. It is usually a time for parties, feasts, and exchanging presents.

The origins of Christmas

Although most historians believe that Jesus was born in the spring, the founders of the early church chose midwinter as the time to celebrate his birth. They knew that people all over northern Europe already had a midwinter festival on December 21, the longest night of the year, and they decided that midwinter would be the right time to celebrate the beginning of Christianity.

Many of our Christmas traditions have their roots in the ancient midwinter festival, when evergreens were used as decorations. In Scandinavia, people used to bring a huge log in from the forest and burn it as an offering to the Sun god. This is the origin of the Yule log that people used to burn in their hearths at Christmas time.

What to eat at Christmas

All around the world there are different traditional foods that people prepare for their big Christmas meal. Cakes and candies are popular in many countries. In some places, such as Hungary and Belgium, these sweets are wrapped in special paper and hung from the branches of the family Christmas tree.

Many German towns have Christmas markets like this one in Frankfurt.

In many countries, the main Christmas meal is served on Christmas Eve. The Christmas recipes in this book come from the countries shown in yellow on the map on page 4.

Ingredients

honey

candied cherries

cloves

apple pie spice

flaked almonds

ground almonds

candied peel

stock cube

cinnamon

nutmeg

Preserved fruit

Many Christmas recipes include cherries, lemon, and orange **peel** that have been preserved in sugar. You can buy **candied** cherries, and other candied fruit, such as mixed peel, from supermarkets. The tradition of using preserved fruit began before people had refrigerators, when it was hard to find fresh fruit in the middle of winter.

Spices

Christmas foods often contain spices such as nutmeg, cinnamon, or cloves. Spices were very popular in the past because food was often eaten when it was no longer fresh. The strong flavor of the spices disguised the taste of the food, even if it was spoiled. Today we know that eating spoiled food is dangerous, but the tradition of using spices in many types of food has continued.

Apple pie spice

There are many different kinds of spices. Sometimes, instead of using a little bit of several different spices, it is easier to use a ready-made mixture of ground spices, which is sold as "apple pie spice." The mixture usually contains cinnamon, coriander, caraway, nutmeg, ginger, and cloves.

Honey

Honey can be dark or light, runny or thick. A recipe will always tell you which type you need. Some recipes might ask you to heat honey or sugar. It is important to have an adult help you with this because heated honey or sugar can become very hot.

Stock

Cooks used to make stock by **boiling** bones for hours and hours. The bones gave the water a rich flavor, and this stock could be used as a base for soups and stews. Today you can buy stock cubes and make instant stock by dissolving them in water. There are meat-, fish-, and vegetable-flavored stock cubes.

Nuts

Many Christmas recipes include nuts. Almonds are very popular, and they can be bought ready-**chopped**, toasted, flaked, or ground. If you toast the nuts in the oven yourself, watch them carefully because they burn very easily.

Some people are allergic to nuts. This means that it is very dangerous for them to eat food with even the tiniest trace of nuts in it. Always check that it is all right for your guests to eat nuts. Never serve food with nuts in it to anyone with a nut allergy.

Before You Start

Kitchen rules

There are a few basic rules you should always follow when you are cooking.

- Ask an adult if you can use the kitchen.
- Some cooking processes, especially **frying**, and those using **boiling** water or **syrup**, can be dangerous. When you see this sign, always ask an adult for help.
- Wipe down any work surfaces before you start cooking, and then wash your hands.
- Wear an apron to protect your clothes, and tie back long hair.
- Be very careful when using sharp knives.
- Never leave pan handles sticking out over the edge of the stove or countertop because you might bump into them and knock the pan over.
- Always wear oven mitts to lift things in and out of the oven.
- Wash fruit and vegetables before you use them.

How long will it take?

Some of the recipes in this book are very quick and easy to make, while others are more difficult and may take longer. The stripe across the top of the right-hand page of each recipe tells you how long it will take to prepare each dish. It also shows you how difficult the dish is to make. Every recipe is marked as being either * (easy), ** (medium), or *** (difficult).

Quantities and measurements

You can see how many people each recipe will serve by looking at the stripe across the top of the right-hand page. You can multiply the quantities if you are cooking for more people, or divide them if you want to make less food.

Ingredients in recipes can be measured in different ways. Metric measurements use grams, liters, and milliliters. Imperial measurements use cups and ounces. This book lists both metric and imperial measurements.

In the recipes, you will see the following abbreviations:

tbsp = tablespoon	oz = ounce	in. = inch
tsp = teaspoon	lb = pound	ml = milliliter
cm = centimeter	g = gram	

Utensils

To cook the following recipes, you will need these utensils (as well as essentials, such as spoons, plates, and bowls):

- **baking parchment**
- baking sheet or tray, preferably non-stick
- cake rack
- 9-in. (20-cm) springform cake pan
- **chopping** board
- **colander**
- food processor or blender
- grater
- heavy frying pan with a lid
- large non-stick saucepan
- measuring cup
- muffin tin
- **ovenproof** dish
- paper towels
- pastry brush (for **glazing**)
- potato masher
- rolling pin and board
- set of cookie or pastry cutters
- sharp knife
- **spatula**
- wax paper
- **whisk**

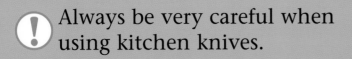 Always be very careful when using kitchen knives.

Shrimp Snacks (Philippines)

The Philippines has a hot, tropical climate. Their Christmas meal is usually a combination of light and tasty snacks. These shrimp fritters are called *ukoy*.

What you need

½ cup (90g) shelled, cooked shrimp
¾ cup (70g) flour
1½ tsp baking powder
1 small garlic clove
1 green onion
1 egg
¼ cup (60ml) water
A pinch of white pepper
Vegetable oil
A pinch of salt

What you do

1 **Chop** the shrimp up into small pieces.

2 Mix flour, baking powder, and salt together in a bowl.

3 Crush the clove of garlic and chop the green onion. Then **beat** the egg and mix it with the garlic and onion. **Season** with pepper.

4 Add ¼ cup (60ml) of water to the egg and onion, then beat this mixture into the flour. It should form a thick, creamy **batter**. If not, add more water, a little at a time, until it forms a batter.

5 Add the shrimp and mix them in well.

6 Pour enough vegetable oil into a heavy frying pan to cover it to a depth of about ¼ in. (1 cm). Turn the heat up under the pan until it is hot enough to make a drop of the batter sizzle.

7 Drop a few spoonfuls of the batter into the pan. Cook for about 2 minutes. Very carefully turn the *ukoy* over with a **spatula.** They should be brown on one side. Cook the other side for about 2 more minutes, until it is brown as well.

8 Take the *ukoy* out of the pan with the spatula and drain them on paper towels. Serve immediately.

SEASONING WITH SOY

Try **sprinkling** a little soy sauce over the *ukoy*. Many people enjoy eating them this way.

Festive Mushroom Soup (Poland)

In Poland the most important Christmas meal is eaten on Christmas Eve, before Midnight Mass, the special communion service that marks the beginning of Christmas Day. It is traditional not to eat meat at this meal. This simple vegetarian soup forms one of several courses.

What you need

1¼ cups (250g) portobello mushrooms
1 large onion
1 tbsp vegetable oil
2 vegetable stock cubes
Juice from ½ of a lemon
⅔ cup (150ml) sour cream
2 **slices** of toasted white or brown bread
1 quart water
1 tbsp parsley, chopped

What you do

1 **Chop** the mushrooms and the onion.

(!) 2 Pour oil into a frying pan. **Fry** mushrooms and onions for about 5 minutes, until the onion is **translucent** and the mushrooms are cooked.

(!) 3 Bring 1 quart water to a **boil** in a saucepan. Add the stock cubes by crumbling them as you add them to the water. Stir until they have dissolved.

4 Add the lemon juice, the cooked onion, and the mushrooms to the vegetable stock.

5 Let the soup **simmer** for about 15 minutes.

6 Take the soup off the heat and add the sour cream, stirring very quickly.

7 Cut the crusts off the toasted bread, then cut into little squares.

8 Serve the soup in bowls, **sprinkling** a few squares of toast and some fresh chopped parsley on top.

Chicken and Meatball Soup (Palestine)

Although most Palestinian people are Muslims, there are many Arab Christians living there, too. This recipe is based on a soup that a Palestinian writer remembers her mother making on Christmas morning.

What you need

2 chicken stock cubes
½ of an onion
½ tsp grated nutmeg
1½ tsp cinnamon
1¼ cup (250g) minced lamb
1 tbsp vegetable oil
¼ cup (50g) long grain rice
1 tbsp tomato **purée**
1 tbsp fresh parsley, chopped
1 quart water

What you do

(!) 1 Make the stock by **boiling** 1 quart of water in a pan and crumbling the stock cubes into it. Turn the heat off, and stir the stock cubes into the water until they have dissolved completely.

2 **Chop** the onion into very fine strips.

3 Mix the onions, spices, and lamb together.

4 Using your clean hands, make the lamb mixture into small meatballs, each one a little bigger than a marble. Wash your hands again.

(!) 5 Heat the oil in a pan, and **fry** the meatballs until they are brown on the outside and cooked through.

14

(!) **6** Reheat the stock until it is boiling, then turn down the heat so that it **simmers** gently. Add the rice, the tomato purée, and the meatballs.

7 Let the soup simmer for about 30 minutes, until the rice is cooked all the way through.

8 Serve the soup in bowls with chopped parsley **sprinkled** over it.

Niños Envueltos (Argentina)

The name of this recipe means "babies in blankets," because that is what it is supposed to look like. It is a good reminder of what Christmas is all about—the birth of baby Jesus.

What you need

½ cup (100g) frozen chopped spinach
Two 4 oz (125g) rump or sirloin steaks
Salt and pepper
1 hard-boiled egg
6 oz (150g) cooked ham
1 tbsp butter
4 sprigs rosemary
1 tbsp flour
1 tbsp vegetable oil
8 oz (227g) can of chopped tomatoes
String

What you do

1 Allow the frozen spinach to **thaw.**

2 Put the spinach in a **colander.** Using a spoon, press it so that as much water as possible is squeezed out.

3 **Season** the meat with salt and pepper.

4 **Chop** up the hard-boiled egg and the ham into very small pieces.

5 Mix the spinach, butter, ham, and egg together. Spoon the mixture onto the pieces of steak.

6 Roll up the pieces of steak. Tie them up and spear each of them with 2 **sprigs** of rosemary.

(!) **7** **Sprinkle** the flour onto a dish and roll the bundles of meat in it until they are entirely coated. Heat the oil in a heavy pan and **fry** the pieces of meat for 1–2 minutes, turning them over at least once. When they are browned, add the tomatoes.

8 Put a lid on the pan, and cook it over low heat for about 20 minutes. Check occasionally to see if it is getting too dry. If it is, add a little water to moisten.

9 Serve one roll to each person.

Savory Rice (Brazil)

This tasty rice recipe is popular on any special occasion in Brazil, including Christmas. Try it with turkey leftovers the day after Christmas, or cook it to go with another South American recipe—the Argentinian recipe for *Niños Envueltos* on pages 16–17.

What you need

1 small onion
½ of a chicken stock cube
½ tbsp olive oil
¾ cup (170g) long grain rice
2 tbsp **chopped**, canned tomatoes
A pinch of salt
1½ cups (350ml) water

What you do

1 **Slice** the onion thinly.

2 Crumble the stock cube into 1½ cups (350ml) of water in a saucepan, and bring to a **boil**.

3 Warm the oil in a large saucepan, tipping the pan to coat the base evenly. Add the onion and **fry** for 5 minutes, or until it is **translucent** but not yet brown.

4 Pour in the rice and stir for 3 minutes, until all the grains are coated with the oil. Do not let the rice turn brown.

5 Add the stock to the rice. Add the tomatoes and salt, and return the mixture to a boil, stirring occasionally.

6 **Cover** the saucepan and turn the heat down low so that the rice is just **simmering**.

7 Cook for 20 minutes or until the rice has **absorbed** all the liquid in the pan.

8 If the rice seems to be drying out, add a little more water and stir well. If it seems to be cooked before 20 minutes, take it off the heat so it does not turn mushy and sticky.

9 Pile the rice onto warm plates and serve immediately.

Jansson's Temptation (Sweden)

In Scandinavia winters are long, dark, and cold. This warm potato dish is traditionally eaten around Christmastime. Anchovies are very small, salty fish that add real flavor to the dish. You can make the recipe without the anchovies, but you should then add some salt along with the pepper.

What you need

1 lb (500g) **waxy potatoes**
1 onion
2 tbsp (25g) butter
8 anchovy fillets, **chopped** (optional)
Black pepper
1 cup (250ml) heavy cream
1 tbsp chopped parsley

What you do

1 **Preheat** the oven to 325°F (160°C).

2 **Peel** the potatoes. Cut them and the onion into thin **slices**.

3 Rub some butter on the inside of an **ovenproof** dish. Use an 8-in. (20-cm) round dish. Set aside the remaining butter.

4 Place a layer of potatoes in the dish, followed by a layer of onions, and a few anchovy fillets. Add another layer of potatoes, continuing until all the potatoes, onions, and anchovies are used up. End with a layer of potatoes.

5 Grind a little black pepper over the potatoes. You will only need to add salt if you have not used anchovies. Pour the cream over the potatoes.

6 Cut the rest of the butter up into small pieces, each about the size of a pea, and scatter these over the potatoes. **Cover** the dish with wax paper.

7 **Bake** the dish for about 45 minutes. Remove the paper and turn the heat up to 350°F (180°C). Bake for another 30 minutes, until the top is golden and the potatoes are cooked through.

8 **Sprinkle** with chopped parsley just before serving.

Mince Pies (England)

Mince pies are served throughout the Christmas season in England. They are little pies filled with a fruit mixture called "mincemeat."

What you need

2 cooking apples
1 tbsp granulated sugar
Juice from 1 orange
1¼ cup (300g) dried, mixed fruit
⅔ cup (150g) butter
¾ cup (150g) brown sugar
¼ cup (30g) mixed **candied** peel
¼ cup (30g) **chopped** almonds
1½ tsp mixed spice
1½ tsp black molasses
2 tbsp flour
1 lb (500g) ready-made pie pastry
A little milk
1 tsp confectioners' sugar
2 tbsp water

What you do

1 **Peel** and core the apples, and then **grate** them.

2 Put the apples in a pan with 2 tbsp of water and all the ingredients, except for the flour, pastry, milk, and confectioners' sugar. **Simmer** until the apples are soft.

3 Put the cooked mixture in a bowl. **Cover** the bowl and put it in the refrigerator. You can use it after 2 hours, but it tastes better after 3 or 4 days.

4 **Preheat** the oven to 400°F (200°C).

5 **Grease** a muffin tin. **Sprinkle** the flour onto a board, and then roll the pastry out as thin as possible. Cut 12 circles and line the holes in the greased tin.

6 Fill each case with mincemeat to the level of the edges of the pastry.

7 Gather up the remains of the pastry. Press it into a ball, then roll it out and cut lids from it by using a slightly smaller cutter. Dampen the edge of each lid with water before pressing it lightly over the filling.

8 Brush each mince pie with milk, then make a small slit in the lid with the point of a knife.

9 **Bake** the mince pies for about 25 minutes, or until they are light golden brown. Sprinkle with sugar.

Ghryba Shortbread (Egypt)

Christians in Egypt celebrate Christmas with many different kinds of **baked** goods, including these shortbread cookies. Egypt's Muslim neighbors use the same recipe to celebrate the end of their annual month of fasting, which is called Ramadan.

What you need

1 cup (200g) butter
¼ cup (60g) confectioners' sugar
1¾ cups (200g) flour
12–15 **peeled**, halved almonds or pine nuts

What you do

1 **Preheat** the oven to 350°F (180°C).

2 Melt the butter in a medium, nonstick pan. Turn off the heat.

3 Add the sugar to the melted butter and mix in well.

4 Using a wooden spoon, add the flour a little at a time, stirring well. Keep adding flour until you have a soft **dough**.

5 By now your dough will be cool enough to handle. Roll it into balls of about the same size as a marble.

6 Flatten the balls of dough out to make small rounds. If the baking sheet is not nonstick, line it with **baking parchment**, and then put the rounds on the sheet.

7 Press an almond or pine nut into the center of each dough round.

8 Bake the dough rounds for about 8 to 10 minutes, until the nuts are browned but the cookies are still a pale cream color. Do not let them turn brown.

9 Cool the cookies on a cooling rack until they are hard and cool enough to eat.

Melomakarona (Greece)

The most important festival of the year in Greece is Easter, but this doesn't mean that Christmas goes by unnoticed. There are always plenty of good things to eat on Christmas Day, such as these little cakes soaked in honey.

What you need

½ cup (125ml) olive oil
½ cup (100g) plus 2 tbsp (25g) granulated sugar
4 tsp (20ml) freshly squeezed orange juice
1/4 cup (185ml) dark, runny honey, plus 1/2 cup (270ml) for syrup
2¾ cups (250g) flour
1/2 tsp apple pie spice
1/2 tsp **grated** orange peel
1 1/2 tsp baking powder
1 tbsp confectioners' sugar
To decorate (optional):
1/4 tsp ground cinnamon and **chopped** walnuts

What you do

1 **Preheat** the oven to 350°F (180°C).

2 **Beat** together the oil, sugar, orange juice, and ¼ cup honey.

3 Mix the flour, spice, orange **peel**, and baking powder together. Add it to the oil and sugar mixture.

4 Mix all these ingredients together in a bowl to form a soft **dough**.

5 Divide the dough into 4 pieces and roll them between your hands to make sausage shapes about 1 in. (2 cm) wide. Cut each sausage shape into sections of about 2 in. (5 cm) long.

(!) **6** Place the shapes on a baking sheet. If the sheet is not nonstick, line it with **baking parchment**. **Bake** for about 30 minutes.

(!) **7** To make the **syrup,** put ½ cup (270ml) honey in a small, nonstick pan, and add ½ cup (100g) granulated sugar. Heat gently until dissolved, and then let the mixture **boil** for about 5 minutes.

8 Remove cakes from the oven, put in a shallow dish, and pour the honey syrup over them. Cool for 5 minutes.

9 Using a **spatula**, put the cakes on a serving plate. **Sprinkle** with confectioners' sugar mixed with ground cinnamon. You can also scatter some walnuts on top.

Stollen (Austria)

Stollen is a Christmas bread. It is meant to look like a baby wrapped in old-fashioned swaddling clothes to remind people of Jesus as a baby.

What you need

Grated peel and juice from a lemon

¼ cup (50g) mixed candied peel

¾ cup (150g) diced, mixed dried fruit

1½ tsp nutmeg

1 cup (200ml) orange juice

2¼ cups (500g) white bread flour

½ cup (100g) granulated sugar, plus ½ cup for glaze

¼ cup (50ml) warm milk

2 tbsp (125g) soft butter

One package quick-acting dry yeast

¼ cup (40g) melted butter

½ cup (100g) marzipan

¼ cup (25g) candied cherries

¼ cup (25g) flaked almonds

½ cup (120ml) plus 2 tbsp water

What you do

1 Put the **candied peel**, fruit, and nutmeg, and about ¾ of the **grated** peel in a pan. Add enough orange juice to cover. Add a little lemon juice.

2 **Simmer** these ingredients together for about 10 minutes, until the liquid is **absorbed**. Let the mixture cool.

3 To make the **dough**, mix the flour, sugar, milk, soft butter, and **yeast** together with ½ cup (120ml) warm water. **Knead** for 10 minutes on a floured board.

4 Put the dough in a bowl and **cover** it with plastic wrap. Put it in a warm place to **rise**, until it has doubled in size. This will take about 30 minutes.

5 Put the dough back on the board and **punch down** before kneading the cooled fruit into it.

6 Divide the dough in half, and roll it into 2 rectangles. Brush each one with melted butter.

7 Cut the marzipan in half and roll each piece into a sausage shape the same width as the dough. Place a piece of marzipan on top of each piece of dough, then fold one side of each loaf over the other to enclose it. Press down on the tops of the loaves with a rolling pin to make sure that the dough is firmly stuck together.

(!) 8 Allow the loaves to rise again for about 30 minutes. **Preheat** the oven to 375°F (190°C). Then **bake** the loaves for about 35 minutes, until golden brown.

(!) 9 While the stollen are baking, dissolve the granulated sugar in 2 tbsp of **boiling** water to make a **glaze**. Paint the glaze on the hot loaves, then **sprinkle** the candied cherries and flaked almonds on top.

Amaretti (Italy)

These almond-flavored biscuits are traditionally made in the south of Italy, where almonds are one of the most important food products.

What you need

2 cups (200g) ground almonds
½ cup (100g) sugar
2 eggs
1½ tsp almond extract or 2 drops almond essence

What you do

1 Mix the almonds and sugar together.

2 Separate the egg yolks from the whites. You can do this by breaking each egg, one at a time, into a bowl, then using a spoon to carefully lift out the yolks.

3 **Whisk** the egg whites until they are stiff.

4 Mix the egg whites and the almond **extract** (or **essence**) together with the almond and sugar mixture.

5 Line a baking sheet with **baking parchment**.

6 Spoon teaspoonfuls of the mixture onto the sheet, making 30 biscuits.

7 Leave the biscuits at room temperature for 2 hours. During this time they will dry out a little. This will make the finished biscuits crispier.

8 **Preheat** the oven to 350°F (180°C).

(!) 9 **Bake** the *amaretti* for about 15 minutes, or until they are light golden in color.

10 Allow the biscuits to cool completely before serving.

PRETTY PRESENTS

Amaretti make a wonderful Christmas present. Wait until they are cool, and then wrap each biscuit in pretty paper before packing them into a decorated tin or box.

Christmas Cookies (Canada)

There are lots of different recipes for cookies—almost every family in North America has its own "traditional" recipe. Some people like to put colored icing or colored sugar sprinkles on their cookies.

What you need

¾ cup (175g) granulated
   sugar
½ cup (115g) butter
1 egg
½ tsp vanilla extract or
   1 drop vanilla essence
1¼ cups (150g) flour
A pinch of salt
¼ tsp baking powder
Colored sprinkles or
   other cake decorations

What you do

1 **Preheat** the oven to 350°F (180°C).

2 **Beat** the sugar and butter together until they are light and fluffy.

3 Break the egg into the bowl with the butter and sugar. Add the vanilla **extract** or **essence** and mix well.

4 Mix the flour, salt, and baking powder together. Add a few spoonfuls of the flour mixture to the egg, sugar, and butter mixture and stir well. Keep adding the flour and stirring until you have a soft **dough**.

5 Roll out the dough on a floured board until it is about ½ in. thick. Use a cookie cutter to cut out different shapes.

(!) **6** Arrange the cookies on a baking sheet, leaving plenty of space between them as they will spread during cooking. Some decorations will need to be put in place before baking. **Bake** for about 8 minutes. Allow the cookies to cool slightly before you add the remaining decorations.

Christmas Bread (Chile)

This bread is traditionally eaten on Christmas Eve, at a meal that brings the pre-Christmas fast to an end. It is very similar to Christmas breads and cakes that are eaten in Europe. This is because so many people from southern Europe settled in South America in the past.

What you need

½ cup (110g) butter
½ cup (110g) granulated sugar
2 eggs
2 cups (225g) flour
½ cup (110ml) milk
1½ tsp baking powder
½ cup (100g) **candied** cherries
½ cup (100g) golden raisins
¼ cup (50g) **chopped** almonds
¼ cup (50g) mixed candied **peel**
Grated peel from 1 lemon

What you do

1 **Preheat** the oven to 300°F (150°C).

2 **Beat** the butter and the sugar together with a wooden spoon until they are light and fluffy.

3 Break the eggs into the bowl one by one and mix well. Add the flour and mix.

4 **Fold in** the remaining ingredients and mix well.

5 Spoon the mixture into a round, **greased**, 9-in. (20-cm) springform cake pan.

(!) **6** **Bake** the bread in the oven for 1 hour and 30 minutes. It is cooked when you can push a toothpick into its center and it comes out clean.

7 Allow the bread to cool for a couple of minutes before removing it from the pan.

8 Allow the bread to cool completely. Serve in **slices.**

Turrón (Spain)

Turrón is a special Christmas dessert from Spain. It is eaten at the end of a big meal on Christmas Eve. The meal starts late—around 9 P.M.—and often includes seafood, meat, and fish. The *turrón* is served last, with coffee.

What you need

4 eggs
2 cups (400g) finely **chopped**, toasted almonds
1 cup (200g) pale, thick honey
1 cup (200g) granulated sugar
A pinch of cinnamon
Wax paper

What you do

1 Separate the egg yolks from the whites. You can do this by breaking each egg, one at a time, into a bowl, and then using a spoon to carefully lift out the yolks.

2 **Beat** the egg whites until they are stiff.

3 Mix in the almonds to make a **paste**.

4 Put the honey into a pan large enough to hold at least 2 quarts. Heat very slowly until it is runny. Honey gets very hot, so be careful not to splash yourself.

5 Add the sugar and continue to heat until it has melted into the honey. Allow the mixture to **boil** slowly. Be sure to have an adult to help you.

6 Add the paste of nuts and eggs to the honey mixture and stir without stopping over low heat for 10 minutes.

7 Line a large, shallow dish or **cover** a plastic chopping board with wax paper. Pour the mixture

on top. Use a nonstick, heatproof **spatula** to spread it out in a thin layer.

8 Allow the mixture to cool. **Sprinkle** it with cinnamon.

9 After about 12 hours, when the *turrón* has set, break it into small pieces and serve.

HOME OF TURRÓN

The province of Alicante, Spain, is home to the Turrón Museum. Here you can learn about the history of this food.

Candied Sweet Potatoes (United States)

Sweet potatoes are now grown in many parts of the world, but they originally came from South America. The best ones are pinky-orange inside, and look similar to fat carrots, not like potatoes at all. They are especially popular in the southern United States.

What you need

5 sweet potatoes
¼ cup (55g) margarine
½ cup (115g) brown sugar
3 tbsp orange juice
A pinch of ground cinnamon
1½ cups (275g) white marshmallows

What you do

1 **Preheat** oven to 350°F (180°C).

2 Wash the sweet potatoes and cut them into thick **slices**.

3 Put the sweet potatoes into a large saucepan with enough water to cover them.

(!) 4 Bring the sweet potatoes to a **boil** and cook them until they are very **tender**. This should take about 15 minutes.

(!) 5 Remove the potatoes from the heat, and ask an adult to help you drain them. Pour them into a large bowl.

6 Mash the sweet potatoes until they are smooth. Stir in the margarine, brown sugar, orange juice, and cinnamon.

7 Spread the potato mixture evenly into a 8- x 12-in. (20- x 30-cm) baking dish. **Sprinkle** with marshmallows.

8 **Bake** until the potatoes are heated through, and the marshmallows have puffed up and turned golden brown. This should take about 30 minutes. Serve hot.

Christmas Pudding Ice Cream (Australia)

Australia is in the Southern Hemisphere. This means that Christmas comes in the middle of the Australian summer. Although some people have the traditional roast turkey, many others prefer a Christmas picnic or a barbecue followed by ice cream or fruit salad.

What you need

1 pint (500ml) vanilla ice cream

¼ cup (50g) ready-mixed dried fruit

½ of a **grated** apple

½ tsp each of cinnamon, nutmeg, and ginger

1½ tsp black molasses

4 **candied** cherries, **chopped**

A squeeze of lemon juice

½ cup (100ml) orange juice

Toasted hazelnuts

What you do

1 Keep the ice cream in the freezer.

2 Put everything except the nuts and the ice cream into a small, nonstick saucepan. The orange juice should just cover the fruit.

3 Bring the mixture gently to a **boil**, stirring all the time. Cook until the liquid is **absorbed** and the fruit is plump. This should take about 10 minutes.

4 Put the mixture into a small bowl, **cover** it with plastic wrap, and put it in the refrigerator overnight.

5 Put a 1-quart bowl in the freezer overnight as well. The next morning, take the ice cream and the bowl out of the freezer. Scoop the ice cream out of its container and into the chilled bowl.

6 Using a fork, quickly stir the fruit mixture into the ice cream. You may have to wait a few minutes until the ice cream is soft enough to mix, but do not let it become runny. You should still have lumps of ice cream mixed with the fruit.

7 Serve the ice cream immediately, scooping it out into bowls. Decorate with a topping of chopped nuts.

Spiced Grape Juice (Germany)

Germany has many outdoor markets at Christmastime, where all sorts of good things are sold for the festive season. A spicy, hot-wine drink called *Glühwein* is sold to help keep out the cold. This version of the drink uses grape juice instead of wine.

What you need

1 orange
1½ tsp cloves
½ of a lemon
1 quart unsweetened
  pure red grape juice
¼ cup (50ml) dark,
  runny honey
2 cinnamon sticks

What you do

1 Cut the orange in half, and then push the cloves into the skin of one half.

2 **Slice** the other half of the orange and the half lemon very thinly. Set aside.

3 Pour the grape juice into the pan. It must either be a nonstick pan or one with an enamel coating. If you use an unlined metal pan, it will spoil the taste of your spiced grape juice.

4 Add the orange with the cloves in it, then the orange and lemon slices.

5 Add the honey, using a wooden spoon. Do not use a metal spoon.

6 Drop in the cinnamon sticks.

(!) **7** Heat the pan until the juice has just begun to **boil**. **Simmer** for 20 minutes.

(!) **8** **Strain** the hot juice into a jug and serve in glasses or mugs. There should be enough for 4 servings.

WAXED FRUIT

Some oranges and lemons are coated in wax before they are sold. This makes them look shinier and more attractive. If you have to use waxed oranges and lemons in this recipe, you may find that some froth forms on top of the juice as you simmer it. Use a wooden spoon to skim this off.

Further Information

Here are some more books that will tell you about Christmas foods and food for other festivals.

Books

Gold, Rozanne. *Christmas 1-2-3*. New York: Stewart, Tabori & Chang, 2002.

Johnson, Kristin. *Christmas Cookies Are for Giving.* Fountain Hills, Ariz.: Tyr Publishing, 2003.

Robertson, Amy Jo. *No-Bake Holiday Recipes*. Uhrichsville, Ohio: Barbour Publishing, Inc., 2003.

Measurements and Conversions

3 teaspoons=1 tablespoon	1 tablespoon=½ fluid ounce	1 teaspoon=5 milliliters
4 tablespoons=¼ cup	1 cup=8 fluid ounces	1 tablespoon=15 milliliters
5 tablespoons=⅛ cup	1 cup=½ pint	1 cup=240 milliliters
8 tablespoons=½ cup	2 cups=1 pint	1 quart=1 liter
10 tablespoons=⅔ cup	4 cups=1 quart	1 ounce=28 grams
12 tablespoons=¾ cup	2 pints=1 quart	1 pound=454 grams
16 tablespoons=1 cup	4 quarts=1 gallon	

Healthy Eating

This diagram shows you what foods you should eat to stay healthy. Most of your food should come from the bottom of the pyramid. Eat some of the foods from the middle every day. Eat only a little of the foods from the top.

Healthy eating at Christmas

A great deal of the food that we eat at Christmas is not very healthy. Many traditional Christmas recipes are full of fat and sugar. Enjoy your Christmas favorites—but remember to leave room for foods that are better for you.

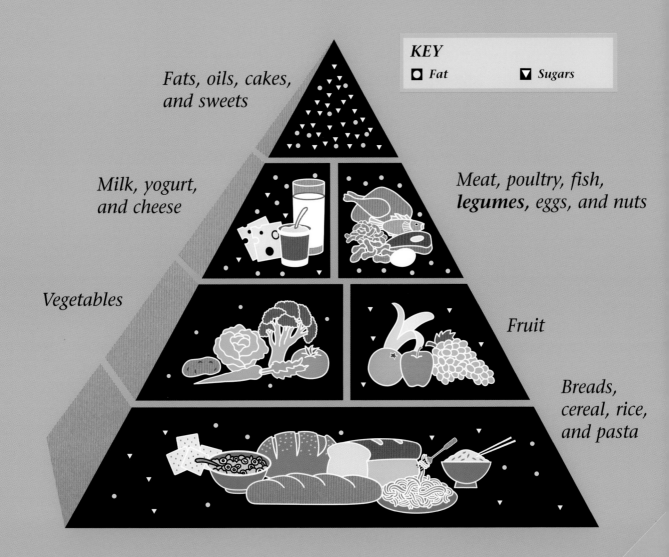

Fats, oils, cakes, and sweets

KEY
◻ Fat   ▽ Sugars

Milk, yogurt, and cheese

Meat, poultry, fish, **legumes**, eggs, and nuts

Vegetables

Fruit

Breads, cereal, rice, and pasta

Glossary

absorb soak up

bake cook something in the oven

baking parchment kind of nonstick paper used to line baking trays or cake pans to prevent food from sticking to them

batter mixture of eggs, milk, and flour used for coating fried foods, or making pancakes

beat mix ingredients together, using a fork or whisk

boil cook a liquid on the stove. Boiling liquid bubbles and steams.

candied cooked in sugar. This is a way of making fruit keep for a long time.

chop cut into pieces using a sharp knife

colander bowl-shaped container with holes in it, used for draining vegetables and straining

cover put a lid on a pan, or put foil or plastic wrap over a dish

dough soft mixture of flour and liquid that sticks together and can be shaped or rolled out. It is not too wet to handle, but it is not dry either.

essence very strong flavoring, such as vanilla or almond essence. It is important not to confuse it with extract—you need only a small drop of essence, while you may need a teaspoonful of extract.

extract flavoring, such as vanilla or almond extract

fold in mix wet and dry ingredients by making cutting movements with a spoon

fry cook something in oil in a pan

glaze coat food with something to make it look glossy. This can be milk, a mixture of beaten egg and milk, or sugar and water.

grate shred something into small pieces using a grater

grease rub fat over a surface to stop food from sticking

knead press and fold with your hands

legume beans, peas, or seeds from plants that often have pods

ovenproof will not crack in the heat of an oven

paste thick mixture

peel remove the skin of a fruit or vegetable; also the skin itself

preheat turn on the oven in advance so that it is hot when you are ready to use it

punch down kneading dough to get rid of big air bubbles. The air bubbles will be smaller when the dough rises for a second time.

purée mash, blend, or liquidize food; or the blended food itself

rise grow bigger. Dough rises when the yeast in it starts to work.

season give extra flavor to food by adding salt, pepper, or other spices

simmer cook liquid on the stove. Simmering liquid bubbles and steams gently.

slice cut something into thin, flat pieces; or the piece of food itself

spatula flat kitchen utensil used to lift and turn things over

sprig small piece of a plant or herb

sprinkle scatter small pieces or drops onto something

strain pour a liquid through a sieve. If a liquid has bits of fruit or flavoring in it, straining can get rid of them.

syrup thick, sweet liquid made from sugar and water

tender soft, but not squashy

thaw defrost something that has been frozen

translucent almost see-through. Onions become translucent when you fry them.

waxy potatoes varieties of potatoes with dense flesh that does not break up when cooked

whisk beat ingredients together to make them light and airy, or the utensil used for doing this

yeast substance used to make bread rise

Index

amaretti 30
Argentina 4, 16
Australia 4, 40
Austria 4, 28

Brazil 4, 18

cakes
    Christmas bread 34
    melomakarona 26
    stollen 28
Canada 4, 32
candied sweet potatoes 38
chicken and meatball soup 14
Chile 4, 34
Christmas bread 34
Christmas cookies 32
Christmas pudding ice cream 40
cookies
    amaretti 30
    Christmas cookies 32
    ghryba shortbread 24

desserts
    candied sweet potatoes 38
    Christmas pudding ice cream 40
drinks
    spiced grape juice 42

Egypt 4, 24
England 4, 22

festive mushroom soup 12

Germany 4, 42
ghryba shortbread 24
Greece 4, 26

Italy 4, 30

Jansson's temptation 20

main courses
    Jansson's temptation 20
    niños envueltos 16
    savory rice 18
mince pies 22

niños envueltos 16

Palestine 4, 14
Philippines 4, 10
Poland 4, 12

savory rice 18
shrimp snacks 10
snacks
    shrimp snacks 10
    turrón 36
soups
    chicken and meatball soup 14
    festive mushroom soup 12
Spain 4, 36
spiced grape juice 42
stollen 28
Sweden 4, 20

turrón 36

United States 4, 38